The Berkshires

Great Barrington to Williamstown

A PHOTOGRAPHIC PORTRAIT

First published in the United States of America by
PilotPress Publishers, Inc.
110 Weschester Road
Newton, Massachusetts 02458
Telephone: (617) 332-0703
http://www.PilotPress.com

and

Twin Lights Publishers, Inc.
10 Hale Street
Rockport, Massachusetts 01966
Telephone: (978) 546-7398
http://www.twinlightspub.com

ISBN 1-885435-25-8

10 9 8 7 6 5 4 3 2 1

Book design by
SYP Design & Production
http://www.sypdesign.com

Cover Photo by: Howard M. Goodman

Printed in China

Other titles in the Photographic Portrait series:

Cape Ann
Kittery to the Kennebunk
The White Mountains
The Mystic Coast, Stonington to New London
The Rhode Island Coast
Upper Cape Cod
Mid and Lower Cape Cod
Boston's South Shore
Naples, Florida
The Champlain Valley
Portland, Maine

ACKNOWLEDGEMENTS

PilotPress Publishers and Twin Lights Publishers would like
to thank the following people for their assistance in prepar-
ing photography captions: Gordon Clark of the
Massachusetts Trustees of Reservations, which owns and
maintains Naumkeag, Bartholemew's Cobble, Monument
Mountain and other carefully preserved sites in the
Berkshires; Lisa Bozzuto, for her assistance in identifying
trees, flowers and shrubbery captured by photographers;
and to historian Bernard Drew, for his remarkable book,
"Great Barrington: Great Town, Great History". Thanks also
to The Berkshire Eagle, for the use of several photographs
that first appeared in its pages.

Our appreciation to Eric and Evelyn Wilska, owners of The
Bookloft in Great Barrington, for their early assistance in
this project.

Thanks for our captions to Ellen G. Lahr. She has worked at
The Berkshire Eagle as a staff reporter for 14 years, and
now serves as the paper's South County Bureau Chief. Her
freelance credits include work for The Boston Globe, New
York Times, and The Philadelphia Inquirer. She lives in
Great Barrington with her husband, John Whalan, and
their two young sons.

To Brenda Swithenbank for continued encouragement and
support.

And finally, this book came about due to the interest, ambi-
tion and commitment of the photographers who ventured
beyond the Berkshires' beaten paths to capture this lovely
region of Massachusetts. A sincere thanks to them for their
efforts and good eyes.

Contents

Introduction

At the westernmost edge of Massachusetts, the Berkshire Hills holds a unique place in New England's history, geography, culture and pristine outdoors. Stretching 81 miles between the Vermont and Connecticut borders, flanking New York to the west, the region is a kaleidoscope of landscapes, people, lifestyles, conventional factory jobs and offbeat careers, historical attractions and scenic adventures. For more than 100 years, the Berkshires has been a mecca for visitors.

At the turn of the last century, many of the wealthiest sojourners here left their own personal monuments: expansive summer "cottages" that rivaled those in Newport, R.I. and the Hamptons. Some, like Naumkaeg, are museums reflecting a time of vast indulgence.

Visitors have become more democratic in their composition, and some eventually decide to put down roots next door to the old timers who have made this place what it is today. The hills beckon urban refugees who are moving to "the country," with their portable jobs in tow, in search of small-town living. Other city people buy second homes—weekend places where they can escape to breath the mountain air.

In every town are families with deep historical roots—families who built up local lumber mills and paper factories, libraries and town halls. They are the people who serve on the town boards—unpaid public officials who run the communities, protect the environment and preserve the towns' histories.

In Southern Berkshire County, tourism is the economic nugget, fanning out in the summer from the musical delights of Tanglewood, summer home of the Boston Symphony Orchestra. Tanglewood is the entree to a smorgasbord of professional summer stock theater, original art created in former paper mills, music clubs crooning blues, folk, jazz and Latino dance music. The back rooms of museums and libraries chronicle the region's people and their hard work in the papermaking, stonemasonry, farming and manufacturing industries.

The county's largest city, Pittsfield, is in a revival mode, after losing thousands of jobs, residents and scores of businesses when the formidable General Electric Co. gradually phased out most of its jobs here. The city is building a new minor league ballpark, and a group of local residents is restoring the old Colonial Theatre—a dusty jewel long neglected. Millions in public and private dollars are helping transform North Street, the city's main thoroughfare. Berkshire Museum is an anchor for downtown, providing programs for children, films and collections showing the Berkshires' past.

Pittsfield's two large lakes, Onota and Pontoosuc, are year-round destination spots for swimmers, boaters and fishermen. Pittsfield State Forest and wildlife sanctuaries beckon hikers, bird watchers and quiet walkers.

To the east and north, the rural Berkshires' unassuming hill towns such as Hinsdale, Peru, Windsor and Savoy, New Ashford and Lanesborough are quieter, less traveled mountain town gems. Here, as in the south, farmers struggle from dawn to dusk to keep their dairy farms alive, and sawmills transform local timber into homes. In towns like these, the news of the day can be had at the general-store counter, the Town Hall steps, or at church on Sunday mornings.

North Adams, historically isolated and economically strained by the loss of its mills and factories, has been given new life. From the sprawling old Sprague Electric Co., the Massachusetts Museum of Contemporary Art has sprung up through what was once an industrial eyesore. As the museum becomes a destination point for visitors who once rarely ventured north of Pittsfield, North Adams' business community rallies to accommodate its new overnight guests, diners and browsers.

Williamstown, North Adams' affluent neighbor, is home to Williams College, a small and prestigious college with all the campus beauty and intellectual riches of an Ivy League school. The Williams College Art Museum and the Sterling and Francine Clark Museum exist nearly side-by-side. Standing over all of Northern Berkshire as if a sentry, Mount Greylock, is the state's largest peak—its hues shifting hourly with the movement of the sun, clouds and wind.

The Berkshires boast ownership of the Norman Rockwell Museum, where the great illustrator's paintings are elegantly displayed. The sculptor Daniel Chester French made Stockbridge his home and studio, which are now open to the public. The Hancock Shaker Village in Pittsfield has preserved the lively, productive and inspiring lifestyle that faded away with the local Shakers.

Come and visit, venture past the main roads as our photographers did, and find the nooks and crannies of the Berkshires that suit you best.

—Ellen G. Lahr

Karen Coates is passionate about photography. She enjoys photographing indoors to create unique visual designs and outdoors to portray art in nature and landscapes. As she captures nature's beauty, her camera is a constant companion on vacations, and for the past three years she has visited New England during the splendor of fall's foliage.

Karen is a member of the North Bethesda Camera Club. Attending the club's presentations by local photographers, workshops, field trips and classes taught by fellow members that have allowed her the opportunity to hone her skills, has energized her interest in photography. Entering monthly photography competitions with the club, Karen has placed in the top three and won many honorable mentions. She has also exhibited her work locally.

FIRST PRIZE

Karen L. Coates

NIKON F2, F/16, 1/125

Which way is up? Fall's arrival at Ashmere Lake in Hinsdale is captured in a perfect mirror image on still water.

Robert V. Behr

MINOLTA SRT 101,
EKTACHROME 100

Winter's grip is relentless in Northern Berkshire. This view is from Bee Hill Road, looking toward Mount Greylock.

Winter View of Mount Greylock

Robert Behr started taking photos when he won an Argus C-3 camera in a Texas bingo game 42 years ago. His equipment is a little better now, and his subjects in the Berkshires are unending. He was an English teacher and track coach in a Delaware high school prior to returning to Williams College, his alma mater. Bob is now retired as Director of Alumni Relations at the college, where his photos are sometimes found in college publications. He is a member of the Berkshire Museum Camera Club and enjoys traveling, largely because it affords so many opportunities for photography.

False Chantarelles

Margareta Thaute's love of travel brought her to the United States from her native Sweden, when she was hired as an airline stewardess. After traveling around the world, she lived and worked in New York. She later moved to the Berkshires with her husband and daughter where she has worked as a real estate agent.

Western Massachusetts' hills, rivers and birch trees, reminds her of the nature of Sweden and inspires her to seriously pursue her lifelong interest in photography.

Margareta's award-winning images have appeared in calendars, newspapers and other publications and have been exhibited in galleries, regionally and nationally in both private and corporate collections.

THIRD PRIZE

Margareta Thaute

NIKON 90S, FUJI VELVIA

Wild mushrooms discovered off the main road to Mount Washington.

Great Barrington to New Marlborough

Great Barrington | Sheffield | Egremont
Sandisfield | New Marlborough

Margareta Thaute

NIKON 90S, FUJI VELVIA

A dirt road in Egremont meanders
past an old, weathered barn.

(previous page)

Margareta Thaute

NIKON 90S, FUJI VELVIA

A palette of colors in earth and
sky melt together in this meadow.

Margareta Thaute

NIKON 90S, FUJI VELVIA

The hay bales of late summer are a lovely sight in the meadows of Baldwin Hill in Egremont. Hay bales mean winter-feed for the livestock.

(opposite)

Mary Gendler

NIKON 8008

Autumn's brilliant glow is captured in the leaves of this proud sugar maple along Monument Valley Road in Great Barrington.

(top)

Margareta Thaute

NIKON 90S, FUJI VELVIA

An Egremont hillside, in a seasonal transition.

(bottom)

Margareta Thaute

NIKON 90S, FUJI VELVIA

A crystal blue sky permeates a shady glen.

(above)

Shayne M. Marquis

MINOLTA MAXXUM 400SI,
FUJI 400 FILM, F/13

Campo de'Fiori is one among
many antiques shops that line
Route 7 in Great Barrington,
a destination town for New
England antiquers.

(opposite, top)

Anna C. Krakforst-Lang

PENTAX K1000, 35MM FILM,
F-STOP 1/16

Monument Mountain Regional
High School, nationally recog-
nized as a "Blue Ribbon School"
rests in the eastern shadow
of Monument Mountain.

(opposite, bottom)

Bruce D. Dellea

NIKON N5005-AF, QUANTARAY
TECH 10, NF AF 70-300 LENS,
AFGA 200 FILM, AUTO EXPOSURE

Eight white-tailed deer, caught in
the lens completely on guard,
pass through a meadow on
Alford Road. The county's deer
population draws hundreds of
hunters to the county in late fall.

Shayne M. Marquis

(left)

MINOLTA MAXXUM 400SI, F/19,
FUJI 400

St. James Episcopal Church on
Main Street in Great Barrington.

(below)

Shayne M. Marquis

MINOLTA MAXXUM 400SI, F/16,
FUJI 400 FILM

Searles Castle in Great
Barrington, an 1880s estate once
owned by Mary Hopkins, is now
home of the John Dewey
Academy, a private secondary
school. The home was originally
named for Edward Searles, Mrs.
Hopkins' interior decorator and
later, her husband.

(opposite)

Shayne M. Marquis

MINOLTA MAXXUM 400SI,
FUJI 400 FILM

St. Peter's Roman Catholic
Church rises up against a rich
blue sky.

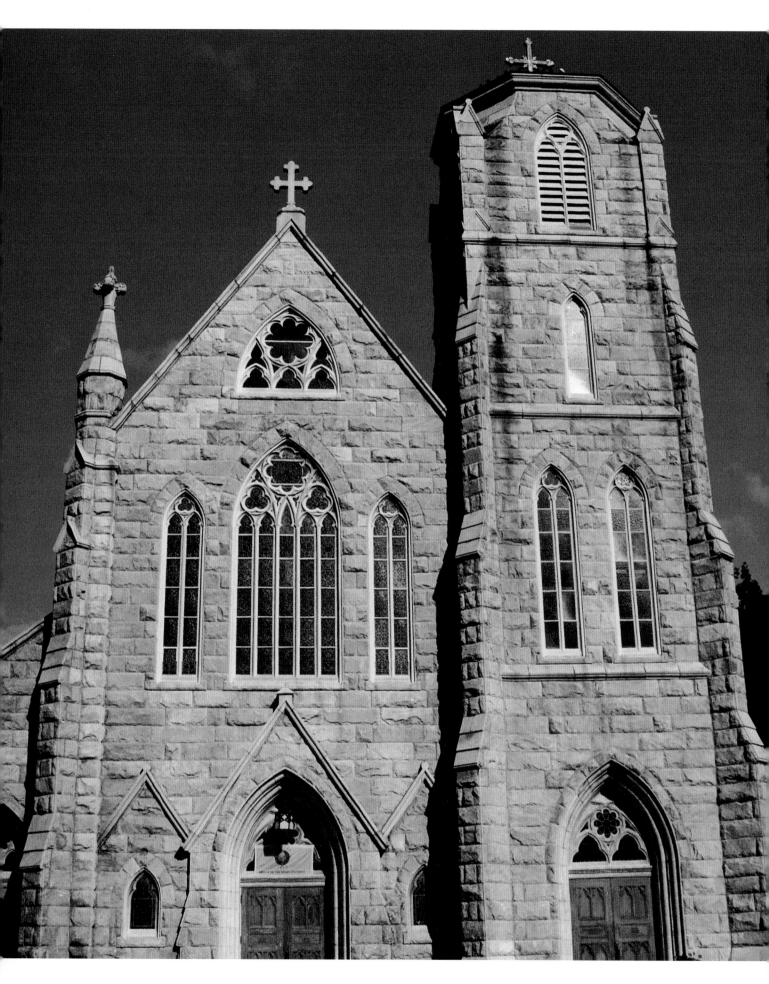

(left)

Shayne M. Marquis

MINOLTA MAXXUM 400SI, FUJI 400 FILM

Simon's Rock College of Bard houses its arts complex and performing arts center in several meticulously preserved New England barns.

(above)

Shannon DeCelle

The Newsboy Monument in Great Barrington is the oldest known statue in the world commemorating news carriers. Col. William Lee Brown, publisher of America's first tabloid newspaper, The New York News, presented the statue to the town on Oct. 10, 1895.

(above)

Shannon DeCelle

Sheffield's landmark covered bridge crosses the Housatonic River near town, linking Main Street with Boardman Street on the opposite shore. The original 19th century bridge was the oldest covered span in Massachusetts until a fire destroyed it in 1994. Bridges were covered in the 19th century to protect their planks from rotting due to rain, snow and moisture.

(opposite)

Shannon DeCelle

A rugged peak at Monument Mountain is a sharp contrast to an evening sunset's soft glow.

(previous page)

Margareta Thaute

NIKON 90S, FUJI VELVIA

A beaver pond in New Marlborough is a pristine mirror for shore and sky.

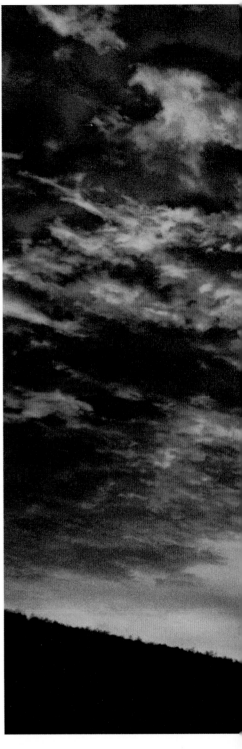

(above)

Eve World

Famed writers Herman Melville and Nathaniel Hawthorne hiked to the peak of Monument Mountain in 1850, and struck up a great literary friendship. The mountain is named for a stone cairn believed created by native Indians who, as legend has it, placed the stones to mark their passing.

(opposite)

Eve World

Bash Bish Falls in Mount Washington is a destination spot for hikers and picnickers seeking the falls' cool mist. There are two hikes into the falls, one an easy stroll, the other a rocky climb only for the sure-footed.

DEVIL'S PULPIT, MONUMENT MT., GREAT BARRINGTON, MASS.   19

ROAD BETWEEN GREAT BARRINGTON AND STOCKBRIDGE, MASS.

(opposite)

Margareta Thaute

NIKON 90S, FUJI VELVIA

Bash Bish Falls.

(above)

Richard Ferrara

VIVITAR XV1, KODAK GOLD 200, F/16, 1/15 EXP.

A long exposure time captures the speed of water rushing along the trail below Bash Bish falls during summer in the town of Mount Washington.

(opposite)

Eve World

The Housatonic River wanders through Bartholomew's Cobble in Ashley Falls. The cobble's unique collection of flora and fauna has brought a state landmark designation to the reservation.

(above)

Shannon DeCelle
The Berkshire Eagle

A summertime swimmer cools off in the Green River in Egremont.

GIBSON'S GROVE, LAKE BUEL, GREAT BARRINGTON, MASS.   82

Andrea Scace

A quiet stand of pines captured in the mirror of a small pond in Sandisfield.

Eve World

April Fool's Day, 1997, brought an early spring snowfall to the area, drooping the boughs of Berkshire firs and delaying eager leaf buds from their spring. Mount Everett rises in the distance.

Eve World

In early summer, wild mountain laurel joins the hillside greenery in higher, rockier elevations with acidic soil. The blooms appear each year around Father's Day.

GREAT BARRINGTON TO NEW MARLBOROUGH **33**

Margareta Thaute

NIKON 90S, FUJI PROVIA F

Snow fences stand against the weather, preventing blowing and drifting snow in critical open areas. The meadow above is on Baldwin Hill in Egremont.

Margareta Thaute

NIKON 90S, FUJI PROVIA F

On Town Hill Road in Egremont, a barn's clinging greenery has gone dormant for the winter.

Margareta Thaute

NIKON 90S, FUJI PROVIA F

At Jug End State Reservation
in Egremont, at the base of
Mount Everett, a stream makes
its determined way through a
snowy field in mid-winter.

Margareta Thaute

NIKON 90S, FUJI PROVIA F

Alford's Village Church reflects
the simple style of early New
England worship spaces.

Stockbridge to Lenox

Stockbridge | West Stockbridge | Richmond
Lee | Tyringham | Lenox

(previous page)

Howard M. Goodman

CANON EOS REBEL 200, E100VS
COLOR SLIDE FILM, F/5.6,
1/750 SEC

Olivia's Overlook on the Lenox-
Richmond town line gives a
lush eastward view over
Stockbridge Bowl.

(opposite, top)

Louis A. Pergola

CANON AE-1, F/16,
KODACHROME SLIDE FILM

Where Main and Church Streets
meet in Stockbridge, a pink gran-
ite column imported from Scot-
land honors The Rev. Jonathan
Edwards, who in 1750 became
second pastor of the First Congregational Church. The monument was presented by Edwards'
descendents in 1873.

(opposite, bottom)

Louis A. Pergola

CANON AE-1, KODACHROME F/16

Musicians get together for a jam
session on Church Street in Lenox
during the annual Apple Squeeze
fall festival, a September ritual.

(above)

Thomas Rotkiewicz

OLYMPUS C-2020 DIGITAL

At the Chesterwood museum,
once home of the late sculptor
Daniel Chester French, a work
studio opens to an elegant piazza
with a southern view. French,
known as "the dean of American
sculptors," is known best for his
famous Abraham Lincoln sculpture in Washington, D.C.

(opposite)

Thomas Rotkiewicz

OLYMPUS C-2020 DIGITAL

An arbor of greenery and a pot of color welcome patrons to Theresa's Stockbridge Café on Main Street. Owner Theresa Sonsini serves lunch and dinner between June and December.

(above)

Howard Goodman

CANON EOS REBEL 2000, KODAK E100V5 COLOR SLIDE FILM, F 5/6 1/750 SEC

A humble work shed at the Berkshire Botanical Garden in Stockbridge.

(above)

Shayne M. Marquis

MINOLTA MAXXUM, 400SI,
FUJI 400 FILM

Stonover Farm, a private
home on Undermountain
Road in Lenox

(left)

Shayne M. Marquis

MINOLTA MAXXUM 400SI,
FUJI 400 FILM

A relic of the past lives on Main
Street in Lee, where H.A.
Johansson 5&10 sells penny
candy, needlework supplies, toys,
fabric, notions and housewares.

(opposite)

Thomas Rotkiewicz

OLYMPUS C-2020 DIGITAL

The "afternoon garden gate" at
Naumkeag in Stockbridge is
watched over by a reproduction
bust of Caesar Augustus. The
"summer cottage," neither
small nor cottage-like, was built
by wealthy New York lawyer
Joseph Choate in 1886 and is
now a museum of the Trustees
of Reservations.

(above)

Melissa Brown

PENTAX K1000, KODAK 400, F/6

A fence mended over and over swings on its hinge outside a Meadow Street barn in Lee.

(left)

Melissa Brown

PENTAX K1000, KODAK 400, F/11

'They can send me to college, but they can't make me think," reads the bumper sticker on this junk car parked off Tyringham Road.

(opposite)

Melissa Brown

PENTAX K1000, KODAK 400, F/6

A tired red barn in South Lee shows its age on a wintry day.

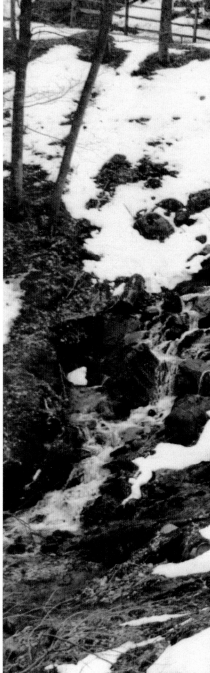

Louis A. Pergola

CANON AE-1, F/16,
KODACHROME SLIDE FILM

A Tyringham house on Main
Road, weathered and sagging
from neglect, awaits a buyer, a
builder or a bulldozer.

Louis A. Pergola

CANON AE-1, F/16,
KODACHROME SLIDE FILM

The Mission House in Stockbridge was built in 1739 for the
Rev. John Sergeant, first mission-
ary to the Mohican and Housatonic Indians. He first lived
among the Indians, but when he
married, his new wife insisted
upon a home of their own. The
house was built on Prospect Hill
but was later moved, piece-by-
piece, to Main Street.

Melissa Brown

PENTAX K1000, KODAK 400, F/8

Tyringham Cobble, a scenic hike that meets up with the Appalachian Trail, crosses this meticulously built stone bridge in Tyringham.

(above)

James J. Selva

NIKON 6006-1000, KODAK
GOLD 200, F/22,

The bridge near the fifth hole at
the Stockbridge Golf Club is no
place for golfers in mid winter.
Cross-country skiers, however,
have made tracks.

(left)

Louis A Pergola

CANON AE-1, F/16,
KODACHROME SLIDE FILM

A winter view in Tyringham
reflects the timelessness of this
idyllic, unspoiled town.

Lynnette Najimy

KALIMAR KX7000
FUJICOLOR SUPERA 800,
F/16, 1/250

The cemetery of the Church-on-the-Hill, which dates back to colonial times, is the resting place of Serge Koussevitzky, Tanglewood's pre-eminent music master.

Shayne M. Marquis

MINOLTA MAXXUM 400SI,
FUJI 400, F/16

The Church-on-the-Hill in Lenox, dedicated in 1805, overlooks the town from its perch at the top of Main Street.

Shannon DeCelle
The Berkshire Eagle

Twilight on Swamp Road in Richmond brings rest to a family farm.

Shayne M. Marquis

MINOLTA MAXXUM 400SI, FUJI 400, F/13

Ripe for the picking, apples await customers at Bartlett's Orchard in Richmond.

Betsy Haynes Rifkin

NIKON FM 24MM LENS, F/8

This ancient resident of Tanglewood, an old spruce, has been around a while. In its old age, it now resembles a Halloween monster.

(top)	(bottom)

Tara Ashley Jones

PENTAX K1000, F/11

Bellefontaine, one of the original summer "cottages" in Lenox, is now Canyon Ranch of the Berkshires, a top-of-the-line luxury spa.

Betty-Jean Collins Cooper

CHINON GENESIS GS-7 REFLEX ZOOM, KODAK 800

The Norman Rockwell Museum in Stockbridge, relocated in 1993 to a 36-acre bluff above the Housatonic River, draws thousands of visitors each year. The famous *Saturday Evening Post* illustrator relied heavily on local residents for models.

Daniel Dougherty

Summer lilies add color to a picket fence in Richmond, where a scruffy, un-pruned apple tree would otherwise rule.

Betty-Jean Collins Cooper

KODAK CAMEO 2X ZOOM PLUS,
KODAK 800 MAX ZOOM FILM

The dormant Stockbridge train
station once received the New
York summer people who traveled here by rail. The pristine station is well preserved, and may
reopen if the freight tracks are
improved to accommodate pas-
senger travel.

The Berkshire Hills, near Chester, Mass.

Daniel Dougherty

Brilliant geraniums decorate the exterior of Charles H. Baldwin & Sons in West Stockbridge, a purveyor of unparalleled vanilla extract, and other flavors since 1888. The store is now run by the fifth generation of Baldwins.

(above)

Shayne M. Marquis

MINOLTA MAXXUM 4000SI, F/4.5
FUJI 400 FILM

The inviting glow inside the
famous Red Lion Inn of
Stockbridge beckons visitors on a
summer's eve. Owned since the
1960's by the Fitzpatrick family
of Stockbridge, the inn dates to
1774 when it was a stagecoach
stop and tavern.

(right)

Shayne M. Marquis

MINOLTA MAXXUM 400SI, F/ 5.6

The Red Lion Inn's Pink Kitty
gift shop.

(top)

Betsy Haynes Rifkin

NIKON 6006, F/8

A string quartet performs at Seiji Ozawa Hall, the most architecturally ornate of Tanglewood's music halls. Crafted mainly of teak and Douglas fir wood, the hall opened in 1994.

(bottom)

Shannon DeCelle

The Sisters of Visitation, whose days are spent in prayerful silence, perform their daily "assignments" in their chapel. A wealthy benefactor enabled the nuns to buy land in Tyringham for a new monastery in the 1990s.

Berkshire Theatre Festival presents
SAY YES!
World Premiere Musical
Music by
WALLY HARPER
...Y BINDER
...ber 2

Shayne M. Marquis

MINOLTA MAXXUM 400SI,
FUJI 400 FILM

Berkshire Theatre Festival in Stockbridge is among the country's finest summer stock theaters, drawing an impressive parade of stage stars each year.

Shannon DeCelle
The Berkshire Eagle

Angelo DiGrigoli takes a spin through downtown Lee during the annual Founders Day celebration. He has lived in Lee for 75 years.

GREENOCK INN, LEE, MASS.

Ellen F. Krupka

OLYMPUS 3000 AUTOMATIC ZOOM

The First Congregational Church in Lee boasts the tallest timber frame steeple in New England. The spire stands 195 feet from sidewalk to steeple top.

(above)

Shayne M. Marquis

MINOLTA MAXXUM 400SI, F/8,
FUJI 400 FILM

The Rookwood Inn's multi-hued
exterior paint job has earned it
the distinction of being a true
"Victorian painted lady." The
Lenox inn was badly damaged in
a 1986 fire, but was beautifully
restored.

(opposite)

Shayne M. Marquis

MINOLTA MAXXUM, F/6.7,
FUJI 400 FILM

Bright, bold storefronts mark the
Main Street in West Stockbridge,
a charming hamlet for artisans of
glass, sculpture and textiles.

(top)

Louis A. Pergola

CANON AE-1, F/16,
KODACHROME SLIDE FILM.

Meadows framed by split rails are a common site on rural back roads. This is Ice Glen Road in Stockbridge, in the early days of fall.

(bottom)

Louis A. Pergola

CANON AE1, KODACHROME
SLIDE FILM

Stockbridge Bowl, still and calm above, comes alive with summer residents, whose homes line the shores. On the distant hillside is the Kripalu Center for Yoga and Health.

Margareta Thaute

Is it fall yet? A sugar maple
answers with its sun-drenched
blaze in Richmond.

(top)

Nancy S. Goldberg

A summer drawing class takes to the lawn at Belvoir Terrace, a summer arts center for budding artists and performers.

(bottom)

Diane L. Marcus

Young dancers Carling Talcott and Kara Buckley pose on the lawn at Belvoir Terrace in Lenox.

Thomas Rotkiewicz

OLYMPUS C-2020 DIGITAL

Hues of blue are gentle on the eyes from Tanglewood's southern lawn. Stockbridge Bowl is in the foreground, with Monument Mountain and distant hills further south.

(above)

Ellen F. Krupka

OLYMPUS 3000 AUTOMATIC ZOOM

At Woods Pond in Lenox, an early morning winter chill is measured by mist, snow and trees stripped bare.

(opposite)

Shannon DeCelle

Solid brick paper mills have endured as a staple of manufacturing in the Berkshires. The Willow Mill in South Lee is a division of Mead Specialty Paper, located about a mile up the river.

Berkshire Cotton Mills and Mt. Greylock,
Adams, Mass.

(above)

Ellen F. Krupka

OLYMPUS 3000 AUTOMATIC
ZOOM

Undermountain Farm in Lenox
invites a picnic on the grass on a
hazy fall afternoon.

(left)

Dan Dougherty

Need milk? High Lawn Farm in
Lee still delivers milk, eggs, cream
and cheese, right to your door.

James J. Selva

NIKON 6006, KODAK GOLD 200, F/5.6

Nature's perfection glistens in this symmetrical hawthorn tree. It is dawn on the green at the Stockbridge Golf Club.

LENOX, Mass. Overlooking Laurel Lake.

Pittsfield to Hinsdale

Pittsfield | Hancock | Dalton | Washington
Windsor | Lanesborough | Peru | Hinsdale

(above)

Shannon DeCelle

Sunset on Pontoosuc Lake in Pittsfield.

(opposite)

Alice Ling

Red maple leaves are among the first to turn each year. These are at Onota Lake.

(previous page)

Howard M. Goodman

CANON EOS REBEL 2000, KODAK E100VS SLIDE FILM, F/5.6, 1/500 SEC.

On Pontoosuc Lake's eastern shore, sailboats at moorings await captains on a summer morn.

(above)

Anne L. White

NIKON N60, KODAK GOLD 100,
F/8, 1/125

Contrasting green mountains
frame the western perimeter of
Onota Lake, where white pines
stand watch.

(opposite)

Anne L. White

NIKON N60, KODAK GOLD, F/8,
1/125

Another view of Onota Lake.

Onota Lake and Potter Mt., Pittsfield, Mass.

(top)	(bottom)
Lenore Esposito	**Lenore Esposito**
SONY DIGITAL	SONY DIGITAL
At Pontoosuc Lake's tall pines offer a perfect welcome to visitors headed for the shore.	A late afternoon on Onota Lake, as seen from nearby Peck's Road.

Andrea Scace

Onota Lake shimmers through the trees along the sloping shore as a walker passes through tall pines.

BATHING, PONTOOSUC LAKE, PITTSFIELD, MASS.

(left)

Shayne M. Marquis

MINOLTA MAXXUM 400SI, FUJI
400 FILM, F/9.5

In Dalton, an ancient Indian
burial site is marked with a
painted rock.

(below)

Shayne M. Marquis

MINOLTA MAXXUM 400SI, F/11,
FUJI 400 FILM

Balance Rock State Forest in
Lanesboro is named for this
unusually situated boulder.

Kristine R. Donovan

MINOLTA MAXXUM 400SLR
AUTOMATIC, KODAK 400 MAX

August is picking time in the blueberry fields of Strawberry Acres farm in Washington.

(top)

Bob Patton

CANON TLB, KODAK 400

These bright purple-pink flowers mark the border of nearly every Berkshire swamp in late summer. This scene is at Springside Park in Pittsfield.

(bottom)

David A. Ellis

NIKON N60, PHOTOWORKS 400 FILM

A spring swallowtail butterfly captured at rest in Washington.

Betsy Haynes Rifkin

NIKON 6006, 85MM LENS, F/5.4

Hearty cattails stand tall among the wildlife surrounding a Pittsfield pond. They will open to reveal a downy white fluff that takes to the wind and spreads the cattail seeds.

(top)

Betty-Jean Collins Cooper

CHINON GENESIS GS-7 REFLEX
ZOOM , 800 MAX ZOOM FILM

The Crane Museum of Papermaking in Dalton exhibits the
history of American papermaking from revolutionary times to
the present. Under heavy security,
Crane & Co. makes the specialty
paper used in U.S. currency.

(bottom)

Patricia J. Sadin

These two new born Romney
lambs cling close to mother
at the Good Shepherd Farm
in Savoy.

(opposite)

Betsy Haynes Rifkin

NIKON 6006, 85MM LENS, F/16

This bird's nest is woven in the
swamp growth around a pond
near Walden Lane in Pittsfield.

Marsha R. Snyder

A remarkable fire of fall color burns on
an island on Pontoosuc Lake in Pittsfield.
A threatening sky augments the bright
trees and mutes the distant hills.

(top)

Daniel Dougherty

Hugh Ferry, a semi-retired farmer, tends to his Windsor hay fields in his 1957 Ford tractor. Ferry gave up his cowherd and sheep flock after the family barn caved in during the spring of 2000.

(bottom)

Daniel Dougherty

A doe and her fawn wander through a backyard in the hill town of Peru.

Josephine Williams

In the village of Berkshire,
between Pittsfield and Lanesboro,
horses graze in early fall.

Mary Ann Palmer

POLAROID

Winter's heavy blanket settles on
the Palmer property on scenic
Washington Mountain Road
in Dalton.

Eve World

On a December day at Hancock Shaker Village, a team of oxen does what comes naturally. The museum includes a working farm that replicates the daily routine of the Shaker community.

Patricia J. Sadin

Sunrise parts the sky over the
Good Shepherd Farm on Griffin
Hill Road, Savoy.

(top)

Shayne M. Marquis

MINOLTA MAXXUM 400SI, F/9.5, FUJI 400 FILM.

On Potter Mountain Road in Hancock, snowy white cows munch the day away.

(botom)

Bill Weisensee

NIKON 2.8, KODAK MAX 400

Black bears pay regular nuisance visits to homes in rural backyards and small town neighborhoods. This rascal has decided it's time to move along after being caught on the deck at a Lanesboro house.

Bradford Swanson

The Hancock Shaker Village museum has preserved the legacy of the Shaker community that lived here from 1790 to 1960. The Brick Dwelling, right, was dormitory for the men and women of the community, and contains an extensive collection of Shaker artifacts and furnishings. The dwelling cost $8,000 to build in the mid 1800s, and used 350,000 bricks.

(top)

Betty-Jean Collins Cooper

KODAK CAMEO 2X ZOOM PLUS,
KODAK 800 MAX ZOOM FILM

Park Square in full bloom.

(bottom)

Shayne M. Marquis

MINOLTA MAXXUM 400SI, F/16,
FUJI 400 FILM

A sun and shade view of Hancock
Shaker Village in Pittsfield.

(top)

Betty-Jean Collins Cooper

KODAK CAMEO 2X ZOOM PLUS,
KODAK 800 MAX ZOOM FILM

The Popcorn Wagon is a Park
Square fixture in the good
weather months, when lunchtime
brings foot traffic to the corner.

(bottom)

Betty Jean Collins-Cooper

KODAK CAMEO 2X ZOOM PLUS,
KODAK 800 MAX

Wally the Stegosaurus greets
visitors at the Berkshire Museum
in Pittsfield. Adopted from a
Cleveland museum, Wally was
named by a Pittsfield boy who
knew of the walnut-sized propor-
tions of the stegosaurus brain.

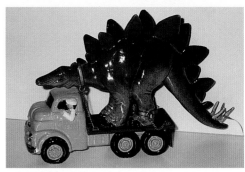

CLAY TOY FROM THE COLLECTION OF
JAMES R. FRANKLIN
SCOTT SCHLEH, ST. AUGUSTINE, FLORIDA

Wally the Stegosaurus caused quite a commotion
as he was transported to the Berkshire Museum.

Betty-Jean Collins Cooper

CHINON GENESIS GS-7 ZOOM,
KODAK 800 MAX ZOOM FILM

Park Square, the gateway into
Pittsfield, has been completely
renovated. The square was
the site of the nation's first
agricultural fair and is now
listed on the National Register
of Historic Places.

(above)

Betty-Jean Collins Cooper

KODAK CAMEO 2X ZOOM PLUS, KODAK 200 FILM

In East Park Cemetery in Pittsfield lies the city's first female settler, Sarah Deming, who later became known as a "pioneer mother of the Revolution."

(left)

Claudia J. Ballen

MINOLTA AF

A summer sunset atop Mount Greylock, where the War Memorial Tower stands. The tower, dedicated in 1933, is lit during three seasons of the year, but is darkened in the fall to prevent confusion among migrating birds.

Shayne M. Marquis

MINOLTA MAXXUM 400SI, F/11,
FUJI 400 FILM

St. Luke's Episcopal Church in
Lanesborough.

Cheshire to Williamstown

Cheshire | New Ashford | Adams
North Adams | Williamstown

(left)

Robert V. Behr

MINOLTA SRT 101, FUJI
SENSIA 100

Thompson Chapel and
Griffin Hall face Main
Street in Williamstown.

(below)

Robert V. Behr

MINOLTA SRT 101, FUJI
PROVIA 100

Near Thompson Chapel at
Williams, students gather
for a seminar on the lawn.
Thompson Chapel was com-
pleted in 1904.

(previous page)

Howard M. Goodman

CANON EOS REBEL 2000, KODAK
E100VS SLIDE FILM, F/5.6,
1/180 SEC.

Early morn rises over a pristine
lake on Pattison Road in North
Adams in early morn.

Robert V. Behr

MINOLTA SRT 101, FUJI
VELVIA 50

West College, built in 1791, was originally a "free school," which two years later became Williams College. Williams is the second oldest college in Massachusetts after Harvard.

Robert V. Behr

MINOLTA SRT 101, FUJI VELVIA 50

The Williams College president's home reflects late Federal-style architecture. Built by the wealthy farmer Samuel Sloan in 1801, the house has been home to college presidents since 1858.

(above)

Margareta Thaute

A summer offering of rolling farmland and uncluttered hills greets motorists driving south of Williamstown. The view is to the east, over the Greylock range.

(right)

Robert V. Behr

MINOLTA SRT 101, FUJI VELVIA 50 FILM

A lush shoreline frames the Green River just south of Williamstown. The symmetrical "V" valley in the distance below Mount Greylock is known as "The Hopper."

(above)

Howard M. Goodman

CANON EOS REBEL 2000,
KODAK E100VS SLIDE FILM, F/5.6,
1/350 SEC.

A stunning sunrise captured just
below the summit of Mount
Greylock, the highest mountain
in Massachusetts at 3,491 feet
above sea level.

(opposite)

Amy Duquette

NIKON N90S, FUJI NPS

Gould Farm, on Gould Road in
Adams, rests near Mount Greylock's base, at Greylock Glen.

Amy Duquette

A blanket of mist in late fall
hangs over an East Road farm
in Adams.

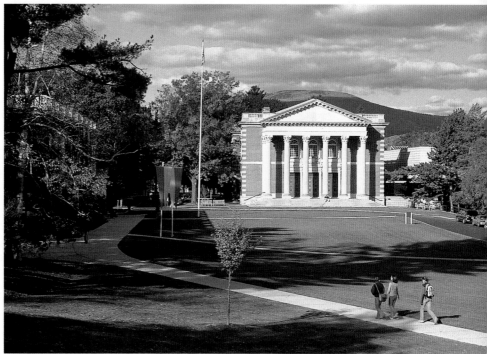

(top)

Robert V. Behr

MINOLTA SRT 101, FUJI
PROVIA 100

Two snow-covered trees frame
stately Griffin Hall, built in 1828
at Williams College.

(bottom

Robert V. Behr

MINOLTA SRT 101, FUJI VELVIA 50

Chapin Hall at Williams is home
to the Berkshire Symphony and
hosts the college's convocations
and other events.

(top)

Robert V. Behr

MINOLTA SRT 101, FUJI
PROVIA 100 FILM

The Green River Valley below
Mount Greylock, just off Scott
Hill Road in Williamstown,
south of town.

(bottom)

Robert V. Behr

· MINOLTA SRT 101, FUJI VELVIA 50

Looking west toward New York
from Mount Greylock's summit,
a hiker can see Mount Prospect
(elev. 2690) in the right foreground and the Taconic Range
in the distance.

Robert V. Behr

MINOLTA SRT 101, FUJI
VELVIA 50.

The War Memorial Tower at
the top of Mount Greylock.
The Appalachian Trail runs past
the base, where Bascom Lodge
serves up Friday night meals to
weary hikers.

(top)

Daniel Dougherty

NIKON 6006 KODAK GOLD 200,
F /5.6

This old Dodge truck in New Ashford is finally ready for retirement.

(bottom)

Robert V. Behr

MINOLTA SRT-101, FUJI
SENSIA 200

Simple sugar shacks like this are a late winter essential for farmers and maple syrup lovers. Williams College students operate this one, in Hopkins Memorial Forest northwest of Williamstown.

Amy Duquette

NIKON N90S, FUJI NPS

Gould Farm, on Gould Road in Adams, rests near Mount Greylock's base, at Greylock Glen.

(top)

Shayne M. Marquis

MINOLTA MAXXUM 400SI, F/16,
FUJI 400 FILM

The old Mohawk Theater anchors downtown's Main Street in North Adams, a blue collar working town where an influx of dot.com companies has earned it the name, "Silicon Village."

(bottom)

Daniel Dougherty

The Williamstown Theatre Festival draws the best and brightest actors and directors to its popular summer stage. Actor Christopher Reeve got his start here; Gwyneth Paltrow, Richard Dreyfus, James Naughton, Richard Chamberlain and Diane Wiest have also graced this stage.

(right)

Eve World

The stately First Congregational Church in Williamstown was built in 1914.

(below)

Shayne M. Marquis

MINOLTA MAXXUM 400SI, F/16, FUJI 400 FILM

Gleaming white against a blue sky, the First Congregational Church in Adams stands watch over the town.

Shannon DeCelle

"UBERORGAN," BY TIM HAWKINSON

Massachusetts Museum of Contemporary Art in North Adams.

(left)

(below)

Robert V. Behr

MINOLTA SRT 101, FUJI ASTIA 100 FILM

A colorful corner of the Williams College president's house gives a lovely view of the town's First Congregational Church spire in the distance.

Shayne M. Marquis

MINOLTA MAXXUM 44SI, F/11,
FUJI 400 FILM

Downtown Adams, merchants
have given a colorful splash to
Center Street, one of the town's
main thoroughfares.

(left)

Alice Ling

Drops of fall color nestle around fungus found on a tree's northern side at Cheshire Cobble in Cheshire.

(below)

Alice Ling

Rocks and ferns live happily together in shady glens like this one at Cheshire Cobble

(above)

Robert V. Behr

MINOLTA SRT 101, FUJI
VELVIA 50 FILM

Neatly stacked for the coming
winter, a few cords of wood are
sheltered under the blaze of fall
in a back yard of the White Oaks
neighborhood of Williamstown.

(right)

Helen Vallencourt

Scattered leaves line the entrance
steps to West College. The Hopkins brothers were early gradu-
ates of Williams, and Mark Hopkins served as a college president.

(above)

Shayne M. Marquis

MINOLTA MAXXUM 400SI, F/16,
FUJI 400 FILM

The Natural Stone Bridge State
Park approach on McCauley
Road in North Adams. The park
includes the only marble dam in
North America.

(opposite)

Shayne M. Marquis

MINOLTA MAXXUM 400SI, F /4.5,
FUJI 400 FILM.

Geological formations at Natural
Stone Bridge State Park. The park
was once an active quarry, and is
now open for tours.

(above

Kim Holzer

NIKON N60, F/90, KODAK
400 FILM

A walking trail at Greylock Glen
passes a popular summer fishing
spot and winter skating location.
Local legend has it that a giant cat-
fish lurks below the surface here.

(left)

Kim Holzer

NIKON N60, F/90, KODAK
400 FILM

Goldenrod bursts to life in
summer at the base of Mount
Greylock in Adams.

Robert V. Behr

MINOLTA SRT 101, FUJI SENSIA 200

Fall finery illuminates the Hopper, with Mount Greylock in the distance. The view is from just off Route 43 south of Williamstown.

WILLIAMSTOWN, MASS. AS SEEN FROM TACONIC TRAIL 108

Contributors

Claudia Ballen
Pittsfield, MA
102

Robert Behr
Williamstown, MA
3, 6, 106 (2), 107, 108, 109, 113 (2),
114 (2), 115, 116, 120, 123, 127

Melissa Brown
New York, NY
46 (2), 47, 49

Karen Coates
Rockville, MD
5

Betty-Jean Collins Cooper
Pittsfield, MA
54, 58–59, 88, 99, 100 (2), 101, 102

Shannon DeCelle
Rensselaer,NY
19, 22, 23, 31, 53, 62, 64,
73, 78, 120,

Bruce Dellea
Alford, MA
15, 25

Kristine Donovan
Pittsfield, MA
85

Daniel Dougherty
Peru, MA
55, 60, 74, 92 (2), 116, 118

Amy Duquette
New York, NY
111, 112, 117

David Ellis
Washington, MA
86

Lenore Esposito
Pittsfield, MA
82 (2)

Richard Ferrara
Amesbury, MA
29

Mary Gendler
Great Barrington, MA
12, 24 (2)

Nancy Goldberg
Lenox, MA
70

Howard Goodman
New City, NY
38–39, 43, 76, 104–105, 110, cover

Kim Holzer
Adams, MA
126 (2)

Tara Ashley Jones
Lee, MA
54

Anna Krakforst-Lang
Canaan, NY
15

Ellen Krupka
Lee, MA
65, 72, 74

Alice Ling
Pittsfield, MA
79, 122 (2)

Diane Marcus
Lenox, MA
70

Shayne Marquis
Stephentown, NY
14, 16 (2), 17, 18, 44 (2), 51, 53,
56 (2), 57, 61, 63, 66, 67, 84 (2),
97, 99, 103, 118, 119, 121, 124, 125

Lynnette Najimy
Pittsfield, MA
51

Mary Ann Palmer
Dalton, MA
94

Bob Patton
Pittsfield, MA
86

Louis Pergola
Richmond, MA
40 (2), 48 (2), 50, 68 (2)

Betsy Haynes Rifkin
Monona, WI
52, 62, 87, 89

Thomas Rotkiewicz
Windsor, CT
41, 42, 45, 71

Patricia Sadin
Savoy, MA
88, 96

Andrea Scace
Pittsfield, MA
32, 83

James Selva
Housatonic, MA
50, 75, 128

Marsha Snyder
Pittsfield, MA
90–91

Bradford Swanson
Pittsfield, MA
98

Margareta Thaute
Alford, MA
1, 7, 8–9, 10, 11, 13 (2), 20–21,
28, 34, 35, 36, 37, 69, 109

Helen Vallencourt
Williamstown, MA
123

Bill Weisensee
Lanesboro, MA
97

Anne White
Pittsfield, MA
80, 81

Josephine Williams
Pittsfield, MA
93

Eve World
Great Barrington, MA
26, 27, 30, 32, 33,
95, 119